Copyright © 2011 XAMonline, Inc.
All rights reserved. No part of the material protected by this copyright notice may be reproduced or utilized in any form or by any means, electronic or mechanical, including photocopying, recording or by any information storage and retrievable system, without written permission from the copyright holder.

To obtain permission(s) to use the material from this work for any purpose including workshops or seminars, please submit a written request to:

XAMonline, Inc.
25 First Street, Suite 106
Cambridge, MA 02141
Toll Free: 1-800-509-4128
Email: info@xamonline.com
Web: www.xamonline.com
Fax: 1-617-583-5552

Library of Congress Cataloging-in-Publication Data

Wynne, Sharon A.
    Minnesota Special Education Core Skills (Birth to Age 21) Practice Test 2:
    Teacher Certification / Sharon A. Wynne. -1st ed.
    ISBN: 978-1-60787-294-8
    1. Minnesota Special Education Core Skills (Birth to Age 21) Practice Test 2
    2. Study Guides   3. MTLE   4. Teachers' Certification & Licensure
    5. Careers

Disclaimer:
The opinions expressed in this publication are the sole works of XAMonline and were created independently from the National Education Association, Educational Testing Service, or any State Department of Education, National Evaluation Systems or other testing affiliates.

Between the time of publication and printing, state specific standards as well as testing formats and website information may change that is not included in part or in whole within this product. Sample test questions are developed by XAMonline and reflect similar content as on real tests; however, they are not former tests. XAMonline assembles content that aligns with state standards but makes no claims nor guarantees teacher candidates a passing score. Numerical scores are determined by testing companies such as NES or ETS and then are compared with individual state standards. A passing score varies from state to state.

Printed in the United States of America   œ-1
Minnesota Special Education Core Skills (Birth to Age 21) Practice Test 2
ISBN: 978-1-60787-294-8

Special Education
Post-Test Sample Questions

1. Howard has been diagnosed as having maladaptive behavior of an immature/anxious withdrawn nature. A behavior that we might expect of Howard, considering his diagnosis is:
   (Rigorous)

   A. Resistance

   B. Teasing

   C. Fantasizing

   D. Hostility

2. Which of these is listed as only a minor scale on the Behavior Problem Checklist?
   (Average)

   A. Motor Excess

   B. Conduct Disorder

   C. Socialized Aggression

   D. Anxiety/Withdrawal

3. Kenny, a fourth grader, has trouble comprehending analogies, using comparative, spatial, and temporal words, and multiple meanings. Language interventions for Kenny would focus on:
   (Rigorous)

   A. Morphology

   B. Syntax

   C. Pragmatics

   D. Semantics

4. Five-year-old Tom continues to substitute the "w" sound for the "r" sound when pronouncing words; therefore, he often distorts words e.g., "wabbit" for "rabbit" and "wat" for "rat." His articulation disorder is basically a problem in:
   (Rigorous)

   A. Phonology

   B. Morphology

   C. Syntax

   D. Semantics

5. **The Carrow Elicited Language Inventory is a test designed to give the examiner diagnostic information about a child's expressive grammatical competence. Which of the following language components is being assessed?**
   (Rigorous)

   A. Phonology

   B. Morphology

   C. Syntax

   D. Both B and C

6. **At what stage of cognitive development might we expect a student to being to think about and systematically consider possible future goals?**
   (Average)

   A. Early Adolescence

   B. Middle Adolescence

   C. Late Adolescence

   D. Adulthood

7. **Which of the following manifestations can be characteristic of students placed in the exceptionality category of Other Health Impaired?**
   (Average)

   A. Limited strength, vitality, or alertness

   B. Severe communication and developmental problems

   C. Chronic or acute health problems

   D. All of the above

8. **A developmental delay may be indicated by a:**
   (Rigorous)

   A. Second grader having difficulty buttoning clothing

   B. Stuttered response

   C. Kindergartner not having complete bladder control

   D. Withdrawn behavior

9. **Which is *least* indicative of a developmental delay?**
   (Rigorous)

   A. Deficits in language and speech production

   B. Deficits in gross motor skills

   C. Deficits in self-help skills

   D. Deficits in arithmetic computation skills

10. An organic reason for mild learning and behavioral disabilities is:
    (Rigorous)

    A. Inadequate education

    B. Toxins

    C. Biochemical factors

    D. Nutrition

11. Of the various factors that contribute to delinquency and anti-social behavior, which has been found to be the weakest?
    (Rigorous)

    A. Criminal behavior and/or alcoholism in the father

    B. Lax mother and punishing father

    C. Socioeconomic disadvantage

    D. Long history of broken home and marital discord among parents

12. Criteria for choosing behaviors to measure by frequency include all but those that:
    (Easy)

    A. Have an observable beginning

    B. Last a long time

    C. Last a short time

    D. Occur often

13. Ryan is three and her temper tantrums last for an hour. Bryan is eight and he does not stay on task for more than ten minutes without teacher prompts. These behaviors differ from normal children in terms of their:
    (Average)

    A. Rate

    B. Topography

    C. Duration

    D. Magnitude

14. The most direct method of obtaining assessment data, and perhaps the most objective, is:
    (Easy)

    A. Testing

    B. Self-recording

    C. Observation

    D. Experimenting

15. Michael's teacher complains that he is constantly out of his seat. She also reports that he has trouble paying attention to what is going on in class for more than a couple of minutes at a time. He appears to be trying, but his writing is often illegible, containing many reversals. Although he seems to want to please, he is very impulsive and stays in trouble with his teacher. He is failing reading, and his math grades, though somewhat better, are still below average. Michael's psychometric (or psycho-educational) evaluation should include assessment for:
(Rigorous)

    A. Mild mental retardation

    B. Specific Learning Disabilities

    C. Mild Behavior Disorders

    D. Hearing Impairment

16. Echolalia is a characteristic of which disability?
(Average)

    A. Autism

    B. Mental Retardation

    C. Social Pragmatic Disorder

    D. ADHD

17. Autism is a condition characterized by:
(Easy)

    A. Distorted relationships with others

    B. Perceptual anomalies

    C. Self-stimulation

    D. All of the above

18. IDEA specified that students with disabilities must be placed in the Least Restrictive Environment (LRE). In the Cascade System of Special Education Services, which of the following would be considered the LRE for a student with a mild learning disability?
(Easy)

    A. A Co-Teach setting

    B. Paraprofessional support in the general education classroom

    C. A separate special education classroom

    D. There is not enough information to make that determination.

19. Requirements for evaluations were changed in IDEA 2004 to reflect that no 'single' assessment or measurement tool can be used to determine special education qualification, recognizing that there was a disproportionate representation of what types of students?
(Average)

    A. Disabled

    B. Foreign

    C. Gifted

    D. Minority and bilingual

20. IDEA identifies specific disability conditions under which students may be eligible to receive special education services. Of the following, which is NOT a specific disability area identified in IDEA?
(Average)

    A. Other Health Impairment

    B. Emotional Disturbance

    C. Specific Learning Disability

    D. Attention Deficit Disorder

21. To be entitled to protection under Section 504, the individual must meet the definition of a person with a disability, which is any person who: 1. has a physical or mental impairment that substantially limits one or more of such person's major life activities, 2. has a record of such impairment, or 3. is regarded as having such impairment. Which of the following is considered a "major life activity"?
(Easy)

    A. Engaging in sports, hobbies, and recreation

    B. Caring for oneself

    C. Driving a car

    D. Having a social network

22. **NCLB and IDEA 2004 changed Special Education Teacher requirements by:**
    (Easy)

    A. Requiring a Highly Qualified status for job placement

    B. Adding changes to the requirement for certifications

    C. Adding legislation requiring teachers to maintain knowledge of law

    D. Requiring inclusive environmental experience prior to certification

23. **Hector is a 10th grader in a program for students with severe emotional disturbances. After a classmate taunted him about his mother, Hector threw a desk at the other boy and attacked him. A crisis intervention team tried to break up the fight, and one teacher hurt his knee. The other boy received a concussion. Hector now faces disciplinary measures. How long can he be suspended without the suspension constituting a "change of placement"?**
    (Rigorous)

    A. 5 days

    B. 10 days

    C. 10 + 30 days

    D. 60 days

24. ***Irving Independent School District v Tatro, 1984,* is significant in its impact upon what component of the delivery of special education services?**
    (Average)

    A. Health Services

    B. FAPE

    C. Speech Therapy

    D. LRE

25. **The family plays a vital role in our society by:**
    (Easy)

    A. Assuming a protective and nurturing function

    B. Acting as the primary unit for social control

    C. Playing a major role in the transmission of cultural values and morals

    D. All of the above

26. **The first American school for students who are deaf was founded in 1817 by:**
    (Easy)

    A. Jean Marc Itard

    B. Thomas Hopkins Gallaudet

    C. Dorothea Dix

    D. Maria Montessori

27. **The movement towards serving as many children with disabilities as possible in the regular classroom with supports and services grew out of:**
    (Average)

    A. The Full Service Model

    B. The Regular Education Model

    C. The Normalization movement

    D. The Mainstream Model

28. **In successful inclusion:**
    (Easy)

    A. A variety of instructional arrangements is available

    B. School personnel shift the responsibility for learning outcomes to the student

    C. The physical facilities are used as they are

    D. Regular classroom teachers have sole responsibility for evaluating student progress

29. **Teaching children functional skills that will be useful in their home life and neighborhoods is the basis of:**
    (Rigorous)

    A. Curriculum-based instruction

    B. Community-based instruction

    C. Transition planning

    D. Functional curriculum

30. **The transition activities that have to be addressed, unless the IEP team finds it uncalled for, include all of the following EXCEPT:**
    (Rigorous)

    A. Instruction

    B. Volunteer opportunities

    C. Community experiences

    D. Development of objectives related to employment and other post-school areas

31. **Which learning theory emphasizes at least seven different ways in which a student learns?**
    (Average)

    A. Cognitive Approach

    B. Ecological Approach

    C. Multiple Intelligences

    D. Brain Based Learning

32. **According to Piaget's theory, a normally developing third grader would be at what stage of development?**
    (Average)

    A. Sensory motor

    B. Pre-Operational

    C. Concrete Operational

    D. Formal Operational

33. **The components that must be included in the written notice provided to parents prior to a proposal or refusal to initiate or make a change in the child's identification, evaluation, or educational placement are: 1. A listing of parental due process safeguards; 2. A description and a rationale for the chosen action; 3. Assurance that the language and content of the notices were understood by the parents; and 4. _____.**
    (Rigorous)

    A. a detailed listing of components that were the basis for the decision

    B. a detailed listing of the Related Services provided by Special Education

    C. a list of the disability areas covered by IDEA

    D. the telephone numbers of local attorneys who specialize in education law

34. When a student is identified as being at-risk academically or socially what does federal law hope for first?
    (Rigorous)

    A. Move the child quickly to assessment

    B. Place the child in special education as soon as possible

    C. Observe the child to determine what is wrong

    D. Perform remedial intervention in the classroom

35. A best practice for evaluating student performance and progress on IEPs is:
    (Rigorous)

    A. Formal assessment

    B. Curriculum-based assessment

    C. Criterion-based assessment

    D. Norm-referenced evaluation

36. Who is responsible for the implementation of a student's IEP?
    (Easy)

    A. Related Service Providers

    B. General Education Teacher

    C. Special Education Teacher

    D. All of the Above

37. The components of effective lesson plan include: quizzes, or review of the previous lesson, step-by-step presentations with multiple examples, guided practice and feedback, and _____.
    (Average)

    A. hands-on projects

    B. manipulative materials

    C. audio-visual aids

    D. independent practice

38. The effective teacher varies her instructional presentations and response requirements depending upon:
    (Easy)

    A. Student needs

    B. The task at hand

    C. The learning situation

    D. All of the above

39. Which of the following is an example of an alternative assessment?
    (Rigorous)

    A. Testing skills in a "real world" setting in several settings

    B. Pre-test of student knowledge of fractions before beginning wood shop

    C. Answering an essay question that allows for creative thought

    D. A compilation of a series of tests in a portfolio

40. Which of the following is NOT an appropriate assessment modification or accommodation for a student with a learning disability?
    (Average)

    A. Having the test read orally to the student

    B. Writing down the student's dictated answers

    C. Allowing the student to take the assessment home to complete

    D. Extending the time for the student to take the assessment

41. Larry has a moderate intellectual disability. He will probably do best in a classroom that has:
    (Average)

    A. A reduced class size

    B. A structured learning schedule

    C. Use of hands-on concrete learning materials and experiences

    D. All of the above

42. In career education, specific training and preparation required for the world of work occurs during the phase of:
    (Easy)

    A. Career Awareness

    B. Career Exploration

    C. Career Preparation

    D. Daily Living and Personal-Social Interaction

43. Which assistive device can be used by those who are visually impaired to assist in their learning?
    (Rigorous)

    A. Soniguide

    B. Personal Companion

    C. Closed Circuit Television (CCTV)

    D. ABVI

44. Marisol has been mainstreamed into a ninth grade language arts class. Although her behavior is satisfactory, and she likes the class, Marisol's reading level is about two years below grade level. The class has been assigned to read *Great Expectations* and write a report. What intervention would be LEAST successful in helping Marisol complete this assignment?
(Average)

    A. Having Marisol listen to a taped recording while following the story in the regular text

    B. Giving her a modified version of the story

    C. Telling her to choose a different book that she can read

    D. Showing a film to the entire class and comparing and contrasting it with the book

45. For which of the following uses are standardized individual tests most appropriate?
(Rigorous)

    A. Screening students to determine possible need for special education services

    B. Evaluation of special education curriculum

    C. Tracking of gifted students

    D. Evaluation of a student for eligibility and placement, or individualized program planning, in special education

46. The Peabody Individual Achievement Test (PIAT) is an individually administered test. It measures math, decoding, comprehension, spelling, and general information, and reports comparison scores. Data is offered on standardization, validity, reliability, and so on. This achievement test has features of a:
(Rigorous)

    A. Norm-Referenced Test

    B. Diagnostic Test

    C. Screening Tool

    D. A and C

47. **Support can be given for all but which of the following facts? IQ scores:**
    (Rigorous)

    A. Are interchangeable but not necessarily consistent between tests of intelligence

    B. Can fluctuate over time periods

    C. Measure innate intelligence

    D. Are single elements of the total abilities attributable to an individual

48. **Which of these would be the least effective measure of behavioral disorders?**
    (Easy)

    A. Projective test

    B. Ecological assessment

    C. Achievement test

    D. Psychodynamic analysis

49. **Anecdotal Records should:**
    (Average)

    A. Record observable behavior

    B. End with conjecture

    C. Record motivational factors

    D. Note previously stated interests

50. **Effective management of transitions involves all of the following EXCEPT:**
    (Rigorous)

    A. Keeping students informed of the sequencing of instructional activities

    B. Using group fragmentation

    C. Changing the schedule frequently to maintain student interest

    D. Using academic transition signals

51. **What is most important to remember when assigning homework?**
    (Average)

    A. Homework should introduce new skills

    B. Homework should be assigned daily

    C. Homework should consist only of practice/review of skills previously introduced in class

    D. Homework should generally take less than thirty minutes to complete

52. After Mrs. Cordova passed out an assignment, Jason loudly complained that he didn't want to do the assignment, laid his head on his desk, and refused to work when requested to do so. Mrs. Cordova ignored Jason and focused on the students who were working on the assignment. Jason eventually began to work on the assignment, at which time Mrs. Cordova approached his desk and praised him for working. What behavior management strategy was Mrs. Cordova implementing? *(Average)*

    A. Proximity control

    B. Assertive discipline

    C. Token economy

    D. Planned ignoring

53. There are students who are unmotivated in the learning environment because of learning problems they have experienced in the past. Some effective ways of helping a student become academically motivated include: *(Average)*

    A. Setting goals for the student and expecting him to achieve them

    B. Avoiding giving immediate feedback, as it may be demoralizing to him

    C. Making sure the academic content relates to personal interests

    D. Planning subject matter based on grade level placement

54. Sam did not turn in any homework on Tuesday or Wednesday morning. Sam's teacher said nothing about it until that Friday, at which time she told him he could not participate in the weekly free activity time because of his zeros in homework for the two days earlier that week. Which characteristic of an effective punisher was violated? *(Easy)*

    A. Intensity

    B. Immediacy

    C. Contingency

    D. All of the above

55. **Which of the following is NOT a feature of effective classroom rules?**
    (Easy)

    A. They are about 4 to 6 in number

    B. They are negatively stated

    C. Consequences are consistent and immediate

    D. They can be tailored to individual teaching goals and teaching styles

56. **In establishing your behavior management plan with the students, it is best to:**
    (Average)

    A. Have rules written and in place on day one

    B. Hand out a copy of the rules to the students on day one

    C. Have separate rules for each class on day one

    D. Have students involved in creating the rules on day one

57. **Shyquan is in your inclusive class, and she exhibits a slower comprehension of assigned tasks and concepts. Her first two grades were Bs, but she is now receiving failing marks. She has seen the Resource Teacher. You should:**
    (Rigorous)

    A. Ask for a review of current placement

    B. Tell Shyquan to seek extra help

    C. Ask Shyquan if she is frustrated

    D. Ask the regular education teacher to slow instruction

58. **The key to success for the exceptional student placed in a general education classroom is:**
    (Easy)

    A. Access to the special aids and materials

    B. Support from the special education teacher

    C. Modification in the curriculum

    D. The general education teacher's belief that the student will profit from the placement

59. Mrs. Freud is a consultant teacher. She has two students with Mr. Ricardo. Mrs. Freud should:
    (Rigorous)

    A. Co-teach

    B. Spend two days a week in the classroom helping out

    C. Discuss lessons with the teacher and suggest modifications before class

    D. Pull her students out for instructional modifications

60. You should prepare for a parent-teacher conference by:
    (Average)

    A. Memorizing student progress/grades

    B. Anticipating questions

    C. Scheduling the meetings during your lunchtime

    D. Planning a tour of the school

Special Education
Post-Test Sample Questions with Rationales

1. Howard has been diagnosed as having maladaptive behavior of an immature/anxious withdrawn nature. A behavior that we might expect of Howard, considering his diagnosis is:
   (Rigorous)

   A. Resistance

   B. Teasing

   C. Fantasizing

   D. Hostility

Answer: C. Fantasizing
Choices A, B, and D are traits of aggressive, acting-out behavior. Choice C, however, is the trait of anxious, withdrawn behavior.

2. Which of these is listed as only a minor scale on the Behavior Problem Checklist?
   (Average)

   A. Motor Excess

   B. Conduct Disorder

   C. Socialized Aggression

   D. Anxiety/Withdrawal

Answer: A. Motor Excess
Motor Excess has to do with over activity, or hyperactivity, in physical movement. The other three items are disorders, all of which may be characterized by excessive activity.

3. Kenny, a fourth grader, has trouble comprehending analogies, using comparative, spatial, and temporal words, and multiple meanings. Language interventions for Kenny would focus on:
(Rigorous)

   A. Morphology

   B. Syntax

   C. Pragmatics

   D. Semantics

Answer: D. Semantics
Semantics has to do with word meanings. Semantic tests measure receptive and expressive vocabulary skills.

4. Five-year-old Tom continues to substitute the "w" sound for the "r" sound when pronouncing words; therefore, he often distorts words e.g., "wabbit" for "rabbit" and "wat" for "rat." His articulation disorder is basically a problem in:
(Rigorous)

   A. Phonology

   B. Morphology

   C. Syntax

   D. Semantics

Answer: A. Phonology

- Morphology is the study of the structure of words and the rules for combining morphemes into words.
- Syntax refers to the set of rules that govern sentence formation and the speaker's understanding of the structure of phrases and sentences.
- Assessment of morphology refers to linguistic structure of words.
- Assessment of syntax includes grammatical usage of word classes, word order, and transformational rules for the variance of word order.

5. The Carrow Elicited Language Inventory is a test designed to give the examiner diagnostic information about a child's expressive grammatical competence. Which of the following language components is being assessed?
(Rigorous)

    A.   Phonology

    B.   Morphology

    C.   Syntax

    D.   Both B and C

Answer: C. Syntax

- Morphology is the study of the structure of words and the rules for combining morphemes into words.
- Syntax refers to the set of rules that govern sentence formation and the speaker's understanding of the structure of phrases and sentences.
- Assessment of morphology refers to linguistic structure of words.
- Assessment of syntax includes grammatical usage of word classes, word order, and transformational rules for the variance of word order.

6. At what stage of cognitive development might we expect a student to being to think about and systematically consider possible future goals?
   (Average)

   A. Early Adolescence

   B. Middle Adolescence

   C. Late Adolescence

   D. Adulthood

Answer: C. Late Adolescence
With some experience in using more complex thinking processes, the focus of middle adolescence often expands to include more philosophical and futuristic concerns, including the following:

- Often questions more extensively.
- Often analyzes more extensively.
- Thinks about and begins to form a code of ethics.
- Thinks about different possibilities and begins to develop own identity.
- Thinks about and begins to systematically consider possible future goals.
- Thinks about and begins to make his or her own plans.
- Begins to think long term.
- Systematic thinking begins to influence relationships with others.

7. Which of the following manifestations can be characteristic of students placed in the exceptionality category of Other Health Impaired?
   (Average)

   A. Limited strength, vitality, or alertness

   B. Severe communication and developmental problems

   C. Chronic or acute health problems

   D. All of the above

Answer: D. All of the above
Other Health Impaired means having limited strength, vitality, or alertness, due to chronic or acute health problems such as a heart condition, tuberculosis, rheumatic fever, nephritis, asthma, sickle cell anemia, hemophilia, epilepsy, lead poisoning, leukemia, or diabetes, which adversely affects a child's educational performance.

8. A developmental delay may be indicated by a:
   (Rigorous)

   A. Second grader having difficulty buttoning clothing

   B. Stuttered response

   C. Kindergartner not having complete bladder control

   D. Withdrawn behavior

Answer: A. Second grader having difficulty buttoning clothing
Buttoning of clothing is generally mastered by the age of 4. While many children have full bladder control by age 4, it is not unusual for "embarrassing accidents" to occur.

9. **Which is *least* indicative of a developmental delay?**
   (Rigorous)

   A. Deficits in language and speech production

   B. Deficits in gross motor skills

   C. Deficits in self-help skills

   D. Deficits in arithmetic computation skills

Answer: D. Deficits in arithmetic computation skills
Arithmetic computation is a specific, learned skill. Developmental delay is a term used for a delay or deficit that is present in many or most cognitive and adaptive areas, not just one academic skill. In a pre-school environment, disabling conditions consistent with a developmental delay are manifested as inability to learn adequate readiness skills, to demonstrate self-help, adaptive, social-inter-personal, communication, or gross motor skills. The most typical symptoms exhibited by school-age students are inattention to tasks, disruptiveness, inability to learn to read, write, spell, or perform mathematical computations, unintelligible speech, an appearance of not being able to see or hear adequately, frequent daydreaming, excessive movement, and, in general, clumsiness and ineptitude in most school-related activities.

10. **An organic reason for mild learning and behavioral disabilities is:**
    (Rigorous)

    A. Inadequate education

    B. Toxins

    C. Biochemical factors

    D. Nutrition

Answer: B. Toxins
Causes for disabilities can primarily be divided into two major categories: organic (biological) and environmental. Under the organic category, prenatal, perinatal, and postnatal factors, genetic factors, biochemical factors, and maturational lag are listed. These are contributors that originate within the body (endogenous).

11. **Of the various factors that contribute to delinquency and anti-social behavior, which has been found to be the weakest?**
    (Rigorous)

    A. Criminal behavior and/or alcoholism in the father

    B. Lax mother and punishing father

    C. Socioeconomic disadvantage

    D. Long history of broken home and marital discord among parents

Answer: C. Socioeconomic disadvantage
There are many examples of choices A, B, and D, where there is socioeconomic advantage.

12. **Criteria for choosing behaviors to measure by frequency include all but those that:**
    (Easy)

    A. Have an observable beginning

    B. Last a long time

    C. Last a short time

    D. Occur often

Answer: B. Last a long time
We use frequency to measure behaviors that do not last a long time. Measures that extend over a long period are better measured by duration.

13. **Ryan is three and her temper tantrums last for an hour. Bryan is eight and he does not stay on task for more than ten minutes without teacher prompts. These behaviors differ from normal children in terms of their:**
    (Average)

    A. Rate

    B. Topography

    C. Duration

    D. Magnitude

Answer: C. Duration
Duration is the length of time a particular behavior continues. Duration is measured by timing the behavior from start to finish.

14. **The most direct method of obtaining assessment data, and perhaps the most objective, is:**
    (Easy)

    A. Testing

    B. Self-recording

    C. Observation

    D. Experimenting

Answer: C. Observation
Observation is often better than testing, due to language, culture, or other factors.

15. Michael's teacher complains that he is constantly out of his seat. She also reports that he has trouble paying attention to what is going on in class for more than a couple of minutes at a time. He appears to be trying, but his writing is often illegible, containing many reversals. Although he seems to want to please, he is very impulsive and stays in trouble with his teacher. He is failing reading, and his math grades, though somewhat better, are still below average. Michael's psychometric (or psycho-educational) evaluation should include assessment for:
    (Rigorous)

    A. Mild mental retardation

    B. Specific Learning Disabilities

    C. Mild Behavior Disorders

    D. Hearing Impairment

Answer: B. Specific Learning Disabilities
Some of the characteristics of persons with learning disabilities are disorder in one or more basic psychological processes involved in understanding or in using spoken or written language that manifests itself in an imperfect ability to listen, think, speak, read, write, spell, or to do mathematical calculations. They cannot be attributed to visual, hearing, physical, intellectual, or emotional handicaps, or cultural, environmental, or economic disadvantage.

16. Echolalia is a characteristic of which disability?
    (Average)

    A. Autism

    B. Mental Retardation

    C. Social Pragmatic Disorder

    D. ADHD

Answer: A. Autism
Echolalia is echoing/repeating the speech of others, which is a characteristic of autism.

17. **Autism is a condition characterized by:**
(Easy)

   A. Distorted relationships with others

   B. Perceptual anomalies

   C. Self-stimulation

   D. All of the above

Answer: D. All of the above
In IDEA, the 1990 Amendment to the Education for All Handicapped Children Act, autism was classified as a separate exceptionality category. It is thought to be caused by a neurological or biochemical dysfunction. It generally becomes evident before age 3. Smith and Luckasson (1992) describe it as a severe language disorder that affects thinking, communication, and behavior. They list the following characteristics:

- **Absent or distorted relationships with people**—inability to relate with people except as objects, inability to express affection, or ability to build and maintain only distant, suspicious, or bizarre relationships.
- **Extreme or peculiar problems in communication**—absence of verbal language or language that is not functional, such as echolalia (parroting what one hears), misuse of pronouns (e.g. he for you or I for her), neologisms (made-up meaningless words or sentences), talk that bears little or no resemblance to reality.
- **Self-stimulation**—repetitive stereotyped behavior that seems to have no purpose other than providing sensory stimulation. This may take a wide variety of forms, such as swishing saliva, twirling objects, patting one's cheeks, flapping one's arms, staring, etc.
- **Self-injury**—repeated physical self-abuse, such as biting, scratching, or poking oneself, head banging, etc.
- **Perceptual anomalies**—unusual responses or absence of response to stimuli that seem to indicate sensory impairment or unusual sensitivity.

18. IDEA specified that students with disabilities must be placed in the Least Restrictive Environment (LRE). In the Cascade System of Special Education Services, which of the following would be considered the LRE for a student with a mild learning disability? *(Easy)*

    A. A Co-Teach setting

    B. Paraprofessional support in the general education classroom

    C. A separate special education classroom

    D. There is not enough information to make that determination

Answer: D. There is not enough information to make that determination
Although choices A, B, or C could provide LRE for some students, decisions must be made according to individual student need, not a disability condition. More information about the student is needed to be able to specify what the student needs and how services can be delivered in the Least Restrictive Environment appropriate to the needs of the individual student.

19. Requirements for evaluations were changed in IDEA 2004 to reflect that no 'single' assessment or measurement tool can be used to determine special education qualification, recognizing that there was a disproportionate representation of what types of students? *(Average)*

    A. Disabled

    B. Foreign

    C. Gifted

    D. Minority and bilingual

Answer: D. Minority and bilingual
IDEA 2004 recognized that there exists a disproportionate representation of minorities and bilingual students and that pre-service interventions that are scientifically based on early reading programs, positive behavioral interventions and support, and early intervening services may prevent some of those children from needing special education services.

20. IDEA identifies specific disability conditions under which students may be eligible to receive special education services. Of the following, which is NOT a specific disability area identified in IDEA?
    (Average)

    A. Other Health Impairment

    B. Emotional Disturbance

    C. Specific Learning Disability

    D. Attention Deficit Disorder

Answer: D. Attention Deficit Disorder
Attention Deficit Disorder is not a separate disability area in IDEA. Students with ADD/ADHD may qualify for special education services under the Other Health Impairment area, if the disability is significant enough to require special education support. Many students with ADD/ADHD receive services through 504; some require no additional support at all.

21. To be entitled to protection under Section 504, the individual must meet the definition of a person with a disability, which is any person who: 1. has a physical or mental impairment that substantially limits one or more of such person's major life activities, 2. has a record of such impairment, or 3. is regarded as having such impairment. Which of the following is considered a "major life activity"?
    (Easy)

    A. Engaging in sports, hobbies, and recreation

    B. Caring for oneself

    C. Driving a car

    D. Having a social network

Answer: C. Driving a car
Major life activities include caring for oneself, performing manual tasks, walking, seeing, hearing, speaking, breathing, learning, and working. While the others may be important to one's quality of life, they are not considered major life activities under 504.

22. **NCLB and IDEA 2004 changed Special Education Teacher requirements by:**
    (Easy)

    A. Requiring a Highly Qualified status for job placement

    B. Adding changes to the requirement for certifications

    C. Adding legislation requiring teachers to maintain knowledge of law

    D. Requiring inclusive environmental experience prior to certification

Answer: A. Requiring a Highly Qualified status for job placement
NCLB and IDEA 2004 place a requirement that all teachers shall be highly qualified to teach in the content areas they teach.

23. **Hector is a 10th grader in a program for students with severe emotional disturbances. After a classmate taunted him about his mother, Hector threw a desk at the other boy and attacked him. A crisis intervention team tried to break up the fight, and one teacher hurt his knee. The other boy received a concussion. Hector now faces disciplinary measures. How long can he be suspended without the suspension constituting a "change of placement"?**
    (Rigorous)

    A. 5 days

    B. 10 days

    C. 10 + 30 days

    D. 60 days

Answer: B. 10 days
According to *Honig versus Doe*, 1988, where the student has presented an immediate threat to others, that student may be temporarily suspended for up to ten school days to give the school and the parents time to review the IEP and discuss possible alternatives to the current placement.

24. ***Irving Independent School District v Tatro, 1984*** **is significant in its impact upon what component of the delivery of special education services?**
    (Average)

    A. Health Services

    B. FAPE

    C. Speech Therapy

    D. LRE

Answer: A. Health Services
IDEA lists health services as one of the related services that schools are mandated to provide to exceptional students. Amber Tatro, who had spina bifida, required the insertion of a catheter on a regular schedule in order to empty her bladder. The issue was specifically over the classification of clean, intermittent catheterization (CIC) as a medical service (not covered under IDEA) or a related health service, which would be covered. In this instance, the catheterization was not declared a medical service, but a related service necessary for the student to have in order to benefit from special education. The school district was obliged to provide the service. The Tatro case has implications for students with other medical impairments who may need services to allow them to attend classes at the school.

25. **The family plays a vital role in our society by:**
    (Easy)

    A. Assuming a protective and nurturing function

    B. Acting as the primary unit for social control

    C. Playing a major role in the transmission of cultural values and morals

    D. All of the above

Answer: D. All of the above
The family is the primary influence in all the roles listed.

26. **The first American school for students who are deaf was founded in 1817 by:**
    (Easy)

    A.   Jean Marc Itard

    B.   Thomas Hopkins Gallaudet

    C.   Dorothea Dix

    D.   Maria Montessori

Answer: B. Thomas Hopkins Gallaudet
In 1817, Thomas Hopkins Gallaudet founded the first American school for students who were deaf, known today as Gallaudet College in Washington, D.C.

27. **The movement towards serving as many children with disabilities as possible in the regular classroom with supports and services grew out of:**
    (Average)

    A.   The Full Service Model

    B.   The Regular Education Model

    C.   The Normalization movement

    D.   The Mainstream Model

Answer: C. The Normalization movement
The Normalization movement advocated movement toward less restrictive environments for people with disabilities. It led to deinstitutionalization and the attempt to let people with disabilities live, go to school, and work in an environment as "normal" or as close as possible to that of their peer group without disabilities.

28. In successful inclusion:
(Easy)

A. A variety of instructional arrangements is available

B. School personnel shift the responsibility for learning outcomes to the student

C. The physical facilities are used as they are

D. Regular classroom teachers have sole responsibility for evaluating student progress

Answer: A. A variety of instructional arrangements is available

Some support systems and activities that are in evidence where successful inclusion has occurred:

Attitudes and beliefs
- The regular teacher believes the student can succeed.
- School personnel are committed to accepting responsibility for the learning outcomes of students with disabilities.
- School personnel and the students in the class have been prepared to receive a student with disabilities

Services and physical accommodations
- Services needed by the student are available (e.g. health, physical, occupational, or speech therapy).
- Accommodations to the physical plant and equipment are adequate to meet the students' needs (e.g. toys, building and playground facilities, learning materials, assistive devices).

School support
- The principal understands the needs of students with disabilities.
- Adequate numbers of personnel, including aides and support personnel, are available.
- Adequate staff development and technical assistance, based on the needs of the school personnel, are being provided (e.g. information on disabilities, instructional methods, awareness and acceptance activities for students and team-building skills).
- Appropriate policies and procedures for monitoring individual student progress, including grading and testing are in place.

Collaboration
- Special educators are part of the instructional or planning team.
- Teaming approaches are used for program implementation and problem solving.

- Regular teachers, special education teachers, and other specialists collaborate (e.g. co-teach, team teach, work together on teacher assistance teams).

Instructional methods
- Teachers have the knowledge and skills needed to select and adapt curricular and instructional methods according to individual student needs.
- A variety of instructional arrangements is available (e.g. team teaching, cross-grade grouping, peer tutoring, teacher assistance teams).
- Teachers foster a cooperative learning environment and promote socialization.

29. Teaching children functional skills that will be useful in their home life and neighborhoods is the basis of:
    (Rigorous)

    A. Curriculum-based instruction

    B. Community-based instruction

    C. Transition planning

    D. Functional curriculum

Answer: B. Community-based instruction
Teaching functional skills in the wider curriculum is considered Community-based instruction.

30. The transition activities that have to be addressed, unless the IEP team finds it uncalled for, include all of the following EXCEPT:
    (Rigorous)

    A. Instruction

    B. Volunteer opportunities

    C. Community experiences

    D. Development of objectives related to employment and other post-school areas

Answer: B. Volunteer opportunities
Volunteer opportunities, although worthwhile, are not listed as one of the three transition activities that have to be addressed on a student's IEP.

31. **Which learning theory emphasizes at least seven different ways in which a student learns?**
    (Average)

    A. Cognitive Approach

    B. Ecological Approach

    C. Multiple Intelligences

    D. Brain Based Learning

Answer: C. Multiple Intelligences
The Multiple Intelligence Theory, developed by Howard Gardner, suggests that students learn in (at least) seven different ways: visually/spatially, musically, verbally, logically /mathematically, interpersonally, intrapersonally, and bodily/kinesthetically.

32. **According to Piaget's theory, a normally developing third grader would be at what stage of development?**
    (Average)

    A. Sensory motor

    B. Pre-Operational

    C. Concrete Operational

    D. Formal Operational

Answer: B. Pre-Operational
Piaget's observations about stages of development have implications for both theories of learning and strategies for teaching. Piaget recorded observations on the following four learning stages: sensory motor stage (from birth to age 2); pre-operational stages (ages 2–7 or early elementary); concrete operational (ages 7–11 or upper elementary); and formal operational (ages 7–15 or late elementary/high school). Piaget believed children passed through this series of stages to develop from the most basic forms of concrete thinking to sophisticated levels of abstract thinking.

33. The components that must be included in the written notice provided to parents prior to a proposal or refusal to initiate or make a change in the child's identification, evaluation, or educational placement are: 1. A listing of parental due process safeguards; 2. A description and a rationale for the chosen action; 3. Assurance that the language and content of the notices were understood by the parents; and 4. _____.

    (Rigorous)

    A. A detailed listing of components that were the basis for the decision

    B. A detailed listing of the Related Services provided by Special Education

    C. A list of the disability areas covered by IDEA

    D. The telephone numbers of local attorneys who specialize in education law

Answer: A. A detailed listing of components that were the basis for the decision

Written notice must be provided to parents prior to a proposal or refusal to initiate or make a change in the child's identification, evaluation, or educational placement. Notices must contain:

- A listing of parental due process safeguards
- A description and a rationale for the chosen action
- A detailed listing of components (e.g., tests, records, reports) that were the basis for the decision
- Assurance that the language and content of the notices were understood by the parents

34. **When a student is identified as being at-risk academically or socially what does federal law hope for first?**
(Rigorous)

    A.	Move the child quickly to assessment

    B.	Place the child in special education as soon as possible

    C.	Observe the child to determine what is wrong

    D.	Perform remedial intervention in the classroom

Answer: D. Perform remedial intervention in the classroom
Once a student is identified as being at-risk academically or socially, remedial interventions are attempted within the regular classroom. Federal legislation requires that sincere efforts be made to help the child learn in the regular classroom.

35. **A best practice for evaluating student performance and progress on IEPs is:**
(Rigorous)

    A.	Formal assessment

    B.	Curriculum-based assessment

    C.	Criterion-based assessment

    D.	Norm-referenced evaluation

Answer: C. Criterion-based assessment
Criterion referenced tests measure a student's knowledge of specific content, usually related to classroom instruction. The student's performance is compared to a set of criteria or a pre-established standard of information the student is expected to know. On these tests, what the student knows is more important than how he or she compares to other students. Examples include math quizzes at the end of a chapter, or some state mandated tests of specific content. Criterion referenced tests are used to determine whether a student has mastered required skills (criteria). As such, they are most appropriate for assessing whether a student has mastered the objectives on an IEP.

36. Who is responsible for the implementation of a student's IEP?
    (Easy)

    A. Related Service Providers

    B. General Education Teacher

    C. Special Education Teacher

    D. All of the Above

Answer: D. All of the above
The Special Education teacher may be the person responsible for writing, distributing, and monitoring progress on the IEP, but all teachers and staff who interact with a child on an IEP are required to follow the dictates of the IEP.

37. The components of effective lesson plan include: quizzes, or review of the previous lesson, step-by-step presentations with multiple examples, guided practice and feedback, and _____.
    (Average)

    A. hands-on projects

    B. manipulative materials

    C. audio-visual aids

    D. independent practice

Answer: D. independent practice
While choices A, B, and C may be written into a lesson plan to supplement any lesson, independent practice that requires the student to produce faster, increasingly independent (reduced scaffolding) responses should be a key component of every lesson plan.

38. **The effective teacher varies her instructional presentations and response requirements depending upon:**
    (Easy)

    A. Student needs

    B. The task at hand

    C. The learning situation

    D. All of the above

Answer: D. All of the above
Differentiated instruction and meeting the needs of the group as a whole must cater to the students' mode of learning to be successful.

39. **Which of the following is an example of an alternative assessment?**
    (Rigorous)

    A. Testing skills in a "real world" setting in several settings

    B. Pre-test of student knowledge of fractions before beginning wood shop

    C. Answering an essay question that allows for creative thought

    D. A compilation of a series of tests in a portfolio

Answer: A. Testing skills in a "real world" setting in several settings
Naturalistic assessment is a form of alternative assessment that requires testing in actual application settings of life skills. The skill of using money correctly could be correctly assessed via this method by taking the student shopping in different settings.

40. Which of the following is NOT an appropriate assessment modification or accommodation for a student with a learning disability?
(Average)

    A.   Having the test read orally to the student

    B.   Writing down the student's dictated answers

    C.   Allowing the student to take the assessment home to complete

    D.   Extending the time for the student to take the assessment

Answer: C. Allowing the student to take the assessment home to complete
Unless a student is homebound, the student should take assessments in class or in another classroom setting. All the other items listed are appropriate accommodations.

41. Larry has a moderate intellectual disability. He will probably do best in a classroom that has:
(Average)

    A.   A reduced class size

    B.   A structured learning schedule

    C.   Use of hands-on concrete learning materials and experiences

    D.   All of the above

Answer: D. All of the above
Depending on the individual needs of the student, all three classroom characteristics could be appropriate.

42. In career education, specific training and preparation required for the world of work occurs during the phase of:
    (Easy)

    A. Career Awareness

    B. Career Exploration

    C. Career Preparation

    D. Daily Living and Personal-Social Interaction

Answer: C. Career Preparation
Curricular aspects of career education include:

- **Career Awareness**—diversity of available jobs
- **Career Exploration**—skills needed for occupational groups
- **Career Preparation**—specific training and preparation required for the world of work

43. Which assistive device can be used by those who are visually impaired to assist in their learning?
    (Rigorous)

    A. Soniguide

    B. Personal Companion

    C. Closed Circuit Television (CCTV)

    D. ABVI

Answer: C. Closed Circuit Television (CCTV)
CCTV is used to enlarge material such as worksheets and books so that it can appear in a readable size.

44. Marisol has been mainstreamed into a ninth grade language arts class. Although her behavior is satisfactory, and she likes the class, Marisol's reading level is about two years below grade level. The class has been assigned to read *Great Expectations* and write a report. What intervention would be LEAST successful in helping Marisol complete this assignment?
(Average)

   A. Having Marisol listen to a taped recording while following the story in the regular text

   B. Giving her a modified version of the story

   C. Telling her to choose a different book that she can read

   D. Showing a film to the entire class and comparing and contrasting it with the book

Answer: C. Telling her to choose a different book that she can read
Choices A, B, and D are positive interventions. Choice C is not an intervention that lets her access the same curriculum as her peers.

45. For which of the following uses are standardized individual tests most appropriate?
    (Rigorous)

    A. Screening students to determine possible need for special education services

    B. Evaluation of special education curriculum

    C. Tracking of gifted students

    D. Evaluation of a student for eligibility and placement, or individualized program planning, in special education

Answer: D. Evaluation of a student for eligibility and placement, or individualized program planning, in special education
In standardized group tests, directions and procedures are carefully prescribed and scripted. Children write or mark their own responses. The examiner monitors the progress of several children at the same time. He cannot rephrase questions or probe or prompt responses. It is very difficult, to obtain qualitative information from standardized group tests. Standardized group tests are appropriate for program evaluation, screening, and some types of program planning, such as tracking. Special consideration may need to be given if there is any motivational, personality, linguistic, or physically disabling factors that might impair the examinee's performance. When planning individual programs, individual tests should be used.

46. The Peabody Individual Achievement Test (PIAT) is an individually administered test. It measures math, decoding, comprehension, spelling, and general information, and reports comparison scores. Data is offered on standardization, validity, reliability, and so on. This achievement test has features of a:
    (Rigorous)

    A. Norm-Referenced Test

    B. Diagnostic Test

    C. Screening Tool

    D. A and C

Answer: D. A and C
Norm-referenced tests compare students with others of his age or grade. It can be used for screening or placement of students.

47. Support can be given for all but which of the following facts? IQ scores: *(Rigorous)*

    A. Are interchangeable but not necessarily consistent between tests of intelligence

    B. Can fluctuate over time periods

    C. Measure innate intelligence

    D. Are single elements of the total abilities attributable to an individual

Answer: C. Measure innate intelligence
IQ scores:

- Do not measure innate intelligence
- Are variable and can change
- Are only estimates of ability
- Reflect only a part of the spectrum of human abilities
- Are not necessarily consistent from test to test
- Are just one sample of behavior, therefore they do not give us all the essential information needed about a student

48. Which of these would be the least effective measure of behavioral disorders?
    (Easy)

    A. Projective test

    B. Ecological assessment

    C. Achievement test

    D. Psychodynamic analysis

Answer: C. Achievement test
An achievement test measures mastery of specific skills. The other tests measure behavior and emotional adjustment.

49. Anecdotal Records should:
(Average)

    A.   Record observable behavior

    B.   End with conjecture

    C.   Record motivational factors

    D.   Note previously stated interests.

Answer: A. Record observable behavior
Anecdotal records should only record observable behavior, describing the actions and not inferences about possible interest or motivational factors that may lead to prejudicial reviews.

50. Effective management of transitions involves all of the following EXCEPT:
(Rigorous)

    A.   Keeping students informed of the sequencing of instructional activities

    B.   Using group fragmentation

    C.   Changing the schedule frequently to maintain student interest

    D.   Using academic transition signals

Answer: C. Changing the schedule frequently to maintain student interest
While you do want to use a variety of activities to maintain student interest, changing the schedule too frequently will result in loss of instructional time due to unorganized transitions. Effective teachers manage transitions from one activity to another in a systematically oriented way through efficient management of instructional matter, sequencing of instructional activities, moving students in groups and by employing academic transition signals. Through an efficient use of class time, achievement is increased because students spend more class time engaged in on-task behavior. These principles are doubly important when working with some learning disabilities.

51. **What is most important to remember when assigning homework?**
    (Average)

    A. Homework should introduce new skills

    B. Homework should be assigned daily

    C. Homework should consist only of practice/review of skills previously introduced in class

    D. Homework should generally take less than thirty minutes to complete

Answer: C. Homework should consist only of practice/review of skills previously introduced in class
The purpose of homework is to practice/review skills previously introduced in class. Homework should never introduce new skills.

52. **After Mrs. Cordova passed out an assignment, Jason loudly complained that he didn't want to do the assignment, laid his head on his desk, and refused to work when requested to do so. Mrs. Cordova ignored Jason and focused on the students who were working on the assignment. Jason eventually began to work on the assignment, at which time Mrs. Cordova approached his desk and praised him for working. What behavior management strategy was Mrs. Cordova implementing?**
    (Average)

    A. Proximity control

    B. Assertive discipline

    C. Token economy

    D. Planned ignoring

Answer: D. Planned ignoring
Mrs. Cordova is using planned ignoring. Planned ignoring means the teacher determines that an inappropriate behavior will be ignored. This often works with attention seeking behaviors. In the ideal situation, once the attention is removed the behavior ceases. It is important, however, to ensure that the student has other more appropriate behavioral options for getting the needed attention available and that the teacher notices them, too.

53. There are students who are unmotivated in the learning environment because of learning problems they have experienced in the past. Some effective ways of helping a student become academically motivated include:
(Average)

   A. Setting goals for the student and expecting him to achieve them

   B. Avoiding giving immediate feedback, as it may be demoralizing to him

   C. Making sure the academic content relates to personal interests

   D. Planning subject matter based on grade level placement

Answer: C. Making sure the academic content relates to personal interests
A student who is unmotivated in a conventional setting may become interested in learning through an individualized program. In such a setting, he can make choices, learn in accordance with his preferred learning style, and participate in pairs or groups, as well as by himself at his own pace.

54. Sam did not turn in any homework on Tuesday or Wednesday morning. Sam's teacher said nothing about it until that Friday, at which time she told him he could not participate in the weekly free activity time because of his zeros in homework for the two days earlier that week. Which characteristic of an effective punisher was violated?
(Easy)

   A. Intensity

   B. Immediacy

   C. Contingency

   D. All of the above

Answer: B. Immediacy
Immediacy was violated, as the punishment was meted out two days after its occurrence. This lapse in time might have rendered it useless or ineffective.

55. Which of the following is NOT a feature of effective classroom rules?
    (Easy)

    A. They are about 4 to 6 in number

    B. They are negatively stated

    C. Consequences are consistent and immediate

    D. They can be tailored to individual teaching goals and teaching styles

Answer: B. They are negatively stated
Rules should be positively stated, and they should follow the other three features listed.

56. In establishing your behavior management plan with the students, it is best to:
    (Average)

    A. Have rules written and in place on day one

    B   Hand out a copy of the rules to the students on day one

    C. Have separate rules for each class on day one

    D. Have students involved in creating the rules on day one

Answer: D. Have students involved in creating the rules on day one
Students are more apt to follow rules when they know the reasons they are in place and took part in creating them. It may be good to already have a few rules pre-written and then discuss whether they cover all the rules the students have created. If not, it is possible you may want to modify your set of pre-written rules.

57. Shyquan is in your inclusive class, and she exhibits a slower comprehension of assigned tasks and concepts. Her first two grades were Bs, but she is now receiving failing marks. She has seen the Resource Teacher. You should:
(Rigorous)

    A. Ask for a review of current placement

    B. Tell Shyquan to seek extra help

    C. Ask Shyquan if she is frustrated

    D. Ask the regular education teacher to slow instruction

Answer: A. Ask for a review of current placement
All of the responses listed above can be deemed correct, but you are responsible for reviewing her ability to function in the inclusive environment. Shyquan may or may not know she is not grasping the work, and she has sought out extra help with the Resource Teacher. Also, if the regular education class students are successful, the class should not be slowed to adjust to Shyquan's learning rate. It is more likely that she may require a more modified curriculum to stay on task and to succeed academically. This would require a more restrictive environment.

58. The key to success for the exceptional student placed in a general education classroom is:
(Easy)

    A. Access to the special aids and materials

    B. Support from the special education teacher

    C. Modification in the curriculum

    D. The general education teacher's belief that the student will profit from the placement

Answer: D. The general education teacher's belief that the student will profit from the placement
All personnel involved with the student must maintain a positive attitude about the success of the student in the general education program. A teacher who has a negative attitude is less likely to provide the appropriate accommodations for the student.

59. Mrs. Freud is a consultant teacher. She has two students with Mr. Ricardo. Mrs. Freud should:
    (Rigorous)

    A. Co-teach

    B. Spend two days a week in the classroom helping out

    C. Discuss lessons with the teacher and suggest modifications before class

    D. Pull her students out for instructional modifications

Answer: C. Discuss lessons with the teacher and suggest modifications before class
Consultant teaching provides the minimum intervention possible for the academic success of the child. Pushing in or pulling out are not essential components. However, an occasional observation as a classroom observer who does not single out any students may also be helpful in providing modifications for the student.

60. You should prepare for a parent-teacher conference by:
    (Average)

    A. Memorizing student progress/grades

    B. Anticipating questions

    C. Scheduling the meetings during your lunchtime

    D. Planning a tour of the school

Answer: B. Anticipating questions
It pays to anticipate parent questions, so you will more likely to be able to appropriately answer the questions. Anticipating the questions the parents may ask can help you plan to topics that need to be addressed in the conference.

ANSWER KEY

1.	C		31.	C
2.	A		32.	B
3.	D		33.	A
4.	A		34.	D
5.	C		35.	C
6.	C		36.	D
7.	D		37.	D
8.	A		38.	D
9.	D		39.	A
10.	B		40.	C
11.	C		41.	D
12.	B		42.	C
13.	C		43.	C
14.	C		44.	C
15.	B		45.	D
16.	A		46.	D
17.	D		47.	C
18.	D		48.	C
19.	D		49.	A
20.	D		50.	C
21.	C		51.	C
22.	A		52.	D
23.	B		53.	C
24.	A		54.	B
25.	D		55.	B
26.	B		56.	D
27.	C		57.	A
28.	A		58.	D
29.	B		59.	C
30.	B		60.	B

RIGOR TABLE

	Easy 27%	Average 35%	Rigorous 38%
Question	12, 14, 17, 18, 21, 22, 25, 26, 28, 36, 38, 42, 48, 54, 55, 58	2, 6, 7, 13, 16, 19, 20, 24, 27, 31, 32, 37, 40, 41, 44, 49, 51, 52, 53, 56, 60	1, 3, 4, 5, 8, 9, 10, 11, 15, 23, 29, 30, 33, 34, 35, 39, 43, 45, 46, 47, 50, 57, 59

www.ingramcontent.com/pod-product-compliance
Lightning Source LLC
LaVergne TN
LVHW061318060426
835507LV00019B/2209